kids tell us

What does the President

real
comments
by
real kids

compiled by
warren hanson and tim nyberg

kids tell us

press

a funny little division of Warren Hanson Organization ?nc.

Kids Tell Us: What Does the President Do?
Copyright ©2004 by Warren Hanson Organization, ?nc. and Tim
Nyberg Creative, Inc.. All rights reserved. No part of this book
may be used or reproduced in any manner whatsoever without
written permission except in the case of brief quotations embod-
ied in critical articles and reviews. For more information please
visit www.kidstellus.com.

Printed in Canada

First printing May, 2004
10 9 8 7 6 5 4 3 2 1

Text: Various kindergarten children, compiled and edited by
Warren Hanson and Tim Nyberg.
Illustrations based on kids' drawings.
Designed by Warren Hanson and Tim Nyberg

ISBN 0-9723539-1-7

Kids Tell Us Press
a funny little division of **W**arren **H**anson **O**rganization, ?nc.
P.O. Box 8100
St. Paul, MN 55108-0100
www.kidstellus.com

This book may be purchased for educational, business, or sales
promotional use. Please contact **www.kidstellus.com** and click
on special sales.

introduction

Kids know lots of things that grown-ups don't. This book, made up entirely of real comments from real kids, tells more about the President than the rest of us could even imagine. — *Warren and Tim*

acknowledgements

We would like to thank the principals, teachers, media specialists, secretaries, and above all, the kindergartners at:

Plainview Elementary, Plainview, MN
Lincoln Center Elementary, S. Saint Paul, MN
Hamilton Elementary, Minneapolis, MN
Triton Elementary, Dodge Center, MN
Roosevelt Elementary, Faribault, MN
Creek Valley Elementary, Edina, MN
Richardson Elementary, N. St. Paul, MN

3

What does the President do?

6

How should
we know?
We don't even
know him!

He calls
everybody
over in a
big blob and
talks.

7

I think he tells people to do something.
He sometimes is a little bossy.

8

He's bossy and he makes people pick the grass.
They put it in a garbage can.

The President
takes away holes
and other stuff we
don't like.
There's no holes
today, but when
there's puddles,
there's kinda like
holes.

9

When he gets papers and they're important and he doesn't want to lose 'em, and then he got a new hat one day and he forgot where he put his hat and those important papers were in there, and he got a new hat.

He carries papers in his hat. 'Cause he doesn't have a backpack.

10

I been to his white house before.
I got to sat on his lap.
And if he had a note in his hat,
I could see it, and he didn't have
any notes in his hat.
(Did he have a hat?)
Mm-hmm. And he had a beard.

The President don't tell jokes.

Presidents never laugh.

He goes to places for work. Like places where he has mediums.

12

I think he practices his ABCs and his numbers.

kids tell us

He rides ponies.

He just rides on a horse with all these other people, doing something for the people, helping 'em.

13

He gets to ride a horse. A little bit at night. And before he goes to his work, a little bit at morning.

Sometimes George
Washington
do's exercise.

Some Presidents
chop up wood.

14

He saves his dogs and
cats out of the tree.

He could go
swimming naked!
Ho Ho, Merry Christmas!

He, like, um,
he writes a note about,
um, he wants to change,
if he wants to change
some rules.
He writes it, and he puts
it in an evelope, and he,
um, he mails it to, um, one
of the other Presidents.

15

Then the other President
mails it to the other
President, and the other
President mails it to the
people. And then people
mails it to other people.

What Does the President Do?

They work on
expensive
papers
and stuff.

16

They write
love letters to
their family or
somewhere.

Sometimes he plays
with the kids and goes
at the park with them.
And he be's nice to
babies and cats.
And also he pats
babies on the head,
and he's nice.

17

He do NOT play with the kids!

He makes
all the
food.

18

No he
doesn't!
He's the
President!

He likes
to run.

He makes money
for himself and
then he gives it to
people.

He speaks
Chinese.

And he makes a mess. In his office, 'cause he couldn't find something, something that was important.

20

A paper. And then he maked a mess. He didn't clean it up, he keeped it that way.
And then he can't find anything!

(What if the
President gets sick?)

I think he'd
get fired.

Then I
will be
President!

21

He makes stuff for people.
Like a teddy bear.

No, Santa does.

(Do Santa and the President know each other?)
Yeah.

22

And the elfs are the
President's friends and
Santa's friends, too.

He might play cards.
With Santa. And the elves.

He might play golf.
With the elves and Santa.

When he goes to work,
he does his writing,
and if somebody gives
him a heart attack
he will turn into a
statue, prob'ly.

23

He's a statue.
He just sits there on a
chair and he's a rock,
and he sits still.

The President makes up stuff.

Some people believe the President.

24

I believe him!

The President
died from a
long time ago,
'cause he had
a fight with
somebody.

25

So that's why
he came into a
statue.
Even he had
wooden teeth.

The President speeches the whole world.

26

He gives speeches to people who watch TV on his channel.

He sleeps in
the day
and works
all night.

He reads
a book to
fourth graders.

28

They help people.

You know, like, make 'em happy.

The President
tells us
everything
he says.

The President
tells important
things.
Like good things
to the people who
are crowded.

Presidents usually work for the Army. I think he leads the line.

30

The Presidents make us happy because some Presidents go to a war. 'Cause some people want George Washington to be their leader.

He holds the
American flag
while they're
fighting
in the war.

31

He protects the
American flag so
people in the war
don't wreck it.

He takes care
of the
American flag.
He keeps it in
a safe place.

32

He sews
the flag.

The pole gets dirty, but not the flag.

33

Sometimes the flag gets old. Then he cleans it, or he throws it away and sews another one.

34

Wherever the
President goes,
he has to
take some
men with him.
So he doesn't
get into any
fights.

Sometimes he sleeps at his work.

Presidents don't get sleepy.

Last time I saw him he was sleeping.

He writes poems and stories.

He plays trains.

36

He plays with dolls or plays outside.

He was in the movie
"Pirates of the
Caribbean."

Both of them!
George Washington
and Abraham Lincoln.

He killed pirates in
the movie because the
President hated the
pirates 'cause they
were made up.

That's a fake story.

All Presidents have a dream.

Couple of them gets bad dreams.

38

He has a lot of good dreams, about us.

He wakes
everybody up.

He has a
pig to wake
everybody up.

40

For his work,
he wants to see
anyone who
wants to be
President too.
Some people
come to see if
he'll let them
be President.

He sits in a chair in a desk.

He turns around in his chair.

41

He walks on his work.

He commands!

He can do whatever he wants.

42

What does the President eat?

44

Salania.

It's this kind of food
that you make.
And there's these
little noodle things
that kind of look
like long white dog
biscuits that you
can put on it.
And when you cook
them, they turn into
noodles.

The President eats
Fruit Loops for
breakfast.

But they're not
regular Fruit Loops.

45

They're golden
Fruit Loops.

He's ordering a pizza.
And I'd say,
"What kind?
Pepperoni or
President pepperoni?"

46

He can't eat pizza
there 'cause there's
none sauce at the
President's house.
And 'cause they don't
got the crust.

I saw the President
at the grocery store.
(What did he have
in his cart?)

Bananas.

He doesn't eat the food that
we eat, he eats different
kind of food. Steak. Turkey.
(Bananas?)

NO! He doesn't EAT that
kinds of food!

He can't eat the food that
we eat. He eats different
kind of food.

I think he likes
five cookies a day
so he don't rot
his teeth.

48

I think the
President doesn't
like a lot of fat.
He like, eats diet
chocolate stuff.

The President eats supper with his wife and his brother and the mayor.

Well, the only way the President eats his food is eating in his office while he works.

Blueberries and macaroni.

Even he eats hotdogs!

50

The President's cake looks like the President's head.

He cooks
marshmallows.

He eats chicken.
He cooks it over
the campfire.

Maybe the
wife cooks
roast beef.

52

(Who makes his food?)

The maid.

(Gee, I don't have a maid!)

The PRESIDENT is who we're talking about! Not you!

He can eat spaghetti.

No, he can't eat bascetti. There's no cheese!

He can't eat candy. The other Presidents won't let him.

They never eated candy and they never made it. They didn't have candy back then.

Where does the President live?

I saw where he lives once. He lives in the governor.

56

He lives in George Washington.

I seen it.
He lives
over there.
But I live
over there.

57

He don't got
neighbors.

58

He lives in a big castle
and he have a
waterfall and a big flag
house. Have a flag on top
of it. I saw it when just
me and my auntie went
to get her driver license.
And I saw his dog. Yeah,
it was cute. It was very
cute, but we couldn't go
over there.
But we saw his house.
It was beautiful.

I know he lives in a
white house.
The house is as
big as a dinosaur.

His house is long
with bars on 'em.

The President, he
lived in a cabin with
a penny on top of it.

(Do you live in a white house?)

Yeah.

(Does the President live there, too?)

60

Yeah, and he plays with us.

I have a house, but he doesn't live with us.

He lives where
he works. In the
kind of white
castle.
And it's big,
and it's not like
a real castle.
It's just kind of
straight.
It just has a
little star
on the top.

He lives in that,
you know, that
yellow cake.
In the steak.
In the steak of
America.
He live in the
yellow one.
(What do they call
the yellow house?)
Banana House.

62

He doesn't live in
the White House.
(What color do
you think his real
house is?)

Red.
The Red House
is a big house.
(How big?)
Fifteen inches.

The President could paint the White House a different color, but he doesn't want to, prob'ly. Because if he painted it a different color, they would have to change the name of it and it would probably be a hard one to remember, and we would prob'ly still be calling it the White House.

His bathtub looks like brown and it has a little color red and, um, and has a little green in the inside of it and a gray, um, ... and he has a microphone inside of it. I seen it! I went there!

He got a toilet and the toilet is white, and got green spots all over it. And he got red on the top.

66

He lives in the Army.
He has a tent.
It's a fancy tent.
It has blankets and
pillows and animals.
Deers and bears and
snakes.
Only the animals
are hanging from the
wall.
On the outside of the
tent, it's always green.

He lives across the lake. One side of the lake and the other side.

He lives in this house that has a bump on the top, and it has windows and has a room.

It's the lighthouse!

68

He really lives
in a white
house,
'cause I always
go past him
when I drive.
When my mom
takes me
somewhere.

The White House is a, um, kinda like a church.

69

He lives with God. Up in the outer space.

70

Somebody lives with him.
All of the other Presidents who aren't dead yet.
Or that are gonna be a President.
There's butlers.
And his wife.

Sometimes they live in a building by the White House. Maybe it's the Green House.

Sometimes he lives in the White House AND the Green House all the time, but he doesn't always live there. He always is on TV.

72

The President can't sell the White House. The next President gets it.

What does the President wear?

He already got socks. He bought a lot of 'em.

74

He got big socks.

He gives his socks to the soldiers.

He wears long
socks and he has
capris.

I think he
wears shoes.

He gots white
socks. His shoes
are black and
they got buckles.

(Do you think the President wears underwear?)

He does, but you don't gotta mention it.

76

He wears nice underwear. With pictures of his kids.

He wears boxers. They are pink and orange and yellow and red. That's all he has!

I think he wears a
black suit and red
boots and he has
red hair.

I think if somebody
falls off of a building,
he catches 'em. Like
Spiderman.
He wears clothes,
but he buys a
costume like that.

He wears a white coat and he has a black suit and a tie, and a hat. He wears it when he goes to the castle.

He prob'ly has a fuzzy coat.

I saw him at Target. He had a big giant hat and a suit on. And he had a name tag.

He wears a
different suit
every day.
But they all look
the same.

They're called
tuxenos.
That's another
word for suit.

The President doesn't get his clothes dirty. His wife flattens them out so they're all clean. She washes them 'cause they get all fuzzy.

80

He wears a sword and a pistol.

When he's not wearing his sword, he keeps it under his bed.

He wears blue and then even he gots yellow that goes off of it on both of his soldiers. And there's like stars on it.

They have dark green spots on their clothes and light green.

Sometimes he sleeps at night, but at morning he goes to work. But not with his wig.

82

He wears kinda like a night gown but it's really not.

He wears a
white wig.

No, he doesn't
wear a wig!

Yes he does!
They wear tall white
wigs. And sometimes
the President comes to
my house.
On Friday he plays
with my baby dog.

They wear wigs. Because the naughty people think they're other people.

84

They wear wigs because they're bald.

George Washington
has a pony on the back
of his head and he has
a wig on it so people
can't see his hair.
Because he might think
that they may laugh,
the people.

85

And they might say
funny things to his hair,
that's why he wears in
a wig.

He has white hair.
And a three-corner
hat.

He has curly hair.

86

All the Presidents
have curly hair.

One President
had black hair.

[As a kid] he still had curly hair. He still had white hair. And still a bow on his head.

In the movie "The Pirates of the Caribbean," he had, like, beads in his hair.

I think the President wear a thoot.

Some suits are, like, blue. And white pants. And yellow buttons.

88

He wears a black uniform with a black and red tie, and a blue shirt under and a yellow thing with his name on it.

Does the President have a Family?

89

He doesn't have a wife. Nobody wants... nobody lives with him. Because prob'ly he be too nice.

90

There's a mom and some kids, and all the things I know is the President.

He lives with his mom and dad, just like we do.

The President
doesn't live with his
mom or dad or
girlfriend or friends!
'Cause I didn't see
'em when I went
there!

I saw a lot of people
that were strangers.
And I saw President
Statue-Head.

He did have
a mother
because...
he's here!

On the news
I heard the
President has
a baby.

(Does the President
have kids?)

Yeah.

(How many?)

Like, three.
Two boys and five
girls.

93

He has six sons.
And one hundred
sisters.

94

The
President,
he has maybe
a President
dad.
And
President
kids.

He has a
girlfriend.

His girlfriend
is rich.
'Cause she
have money!

(Who's in his family?)
His mom and dad and sister and brother and Lincoln, and the butler.

96

His family is all the other Presidents.

He doesn't have a family.

Yeah, his family died. 'Cause the carriage got on fire. But his family's up there watching him. In heaven.

The friends are still alive, too. So he's not alone anymore.

He has thousands of kids.

He has to have a wife if he has kids.
(What is the President's wife's name?)
Mary Rosie.

98

And a baby.
(What is the President's baby's name?)
Michael. His last name is Washington.

A couple of the other Presidents are his brothers.

All the other Presidents have moms.

I know his daughter has brown hair.

He has a wife and the wife build the American flag.

100

What does the President do in his spare time?

Somebody buries
his whole body
and he tries to
get out and he
can't.

102

(Have you ever
done that?)

I haven't buried
the President,
I buried Dean.

He swims at
Camp David.

He swims
in the sand.

Well, I go swimmin' a lot,
and sometimes I see him
when I'm going swimmin'.
But I don't see him very
often when I'm swimmin'.
I just see him a couple
times when I go swimmin'.

They always watch Fred
Flintstone.
I think some of 'em
watch Fred Flintstone
and some of 'em don't.
And then they just, then
they have their lunch in
their little lunch box.
It's just, like, metal with,
um, stars, American flag
on it.

I think he watch HBO.

I think he goes on a walk with someone. Maybe a puppy.

For fun, he goes sledding.

He might surfboard!

Maybe the President has fun when he washes his clothes and it overflows and he skates on the bubbles.

What Does the President Do?

106

The President has his own movie theater. And he makes his own popcorn in his pants.

He ride a airplane to
the beach and ride a
shark. And then the shark
eat the other shark, and
then the shark eat the
other shark with the
President on it, and the
President runs in the
water.

If he gets all his work
done, then he can tan
on the deck.
Or go fishing.

If he don't get work, then he work in the house.

He might go to Florida.
(How do you know?)
Because I've seen a black man in a black coat.

He prob'ly goes to
Montana. I went there,
but he prob'ly went
before me, 'cause
I went to see the
whitecaps and stuff.

He doesn't go to Arizona.

Maybe he goes to
Pennsylvania.
He might look at the
shiny pencil sharpener.

110

All the Presidents...
one of them were
the first President,
and some go to
Pennsylvania and
some go to another
place I don't know,
but, they do a lot
of stuff, but they're
own busy and they
gotta get to work.

The President, all
the time he takes lots
of breaks and walks
his dog and sometimes
swims in his own pool,
and sometimes his dog
jumps in the pool and
joins him.

111

He goes park hopping.
It means that he goes
to lots of parks with his
little girl and baby.

He gets some sleep.
That way if the next
day he gots work he'll
be all sleepy up.

112

On his day off he
sometimes goes to
Canada.

Only on President's
Day he gets a day off,
I think.

He also goes to run
when he has a day off,
and he goes gets drunk.
I don't know… maybe
he does!

He builds sand castles
with his little girl.

On Saturday, he still
has to work. So he can
make a lot of money.

114

Can I have a different question?

Does the President have any pets?

The President has pets. He has a fish named Franklin.

He might have a cat and a dog! His dog's name is... mmm... it's a girl! Named Lexie.

The President's dog's name is Festus. Or Shotski.

I think the dog's name is CJ.

(What's his cat's name?) He's a boy, of course. I think it's Poochie.

I think the cat's name is Charcoal.
(What color is the cat?)
Orange.

He keeps pigs in his big yellow jet, far, far away.

118

The President doesn't even have pigs. He doesn't know what pigs are!

THE PRESIDENT DOESN'T HAVE A PET OR A GIRL FRIEND!!

(How do you know?)

I got to sit on the President's lap and play with a boy there.

The President has a parrot.

I think the parrot's name is Talk.

120

They have white cats.

There might be some kittens!

He's allergic to cats.

He also has a
bunny that hops
all the way around
his office.

Sometimes when
he's afraid of the
dog, the cat climbs
on top of the
President's head.

Actually the President's wife has her own horse.

122

And Abraham Lincoln, he had a horse, and there was this little carrier that would carry him around. Wooden and wheels, four wheels. He sat in the cart.

George Washington,
he had a horse and he
had a sword and he
fights with the other
President.

Sometimes the
President's animals go
by the war and
sometimes their
animals get killed by
the war.
Even the cats.

He has mean dogs to protect him when he's walking his dogs.

124

What kind of rules does the President make?

(How does the President make laws?)

They make it out of logs.

There's lots of people who do stuff wrong, so it's a big book so he makes all the laws in it.

If somebody does it, and he says, "You can't do that!" Then it's a law.

He's the President,
and he tells all the
people to tell the
people not to do that,
and then do that.

He makes sure that
you do good stuff.
Like play together.
And no hitting.

He can build the laws
with bricks.

What Does the President Do?

The President says,
"Don't point!"

Sometimes he tells
people that, there's
always one law that you
should never do... never
kill or smoke.

128

Not to chase other kids
away from parks, or
don't be mean.

He chooses the games
we have to play.

He'll punish you if
you break in the glass
of a car.

The President always
wants you to wash
your teeth.

Never put a
vacuum in
your ear.

What Does the President Do?

When you swear,
that's a law.

When you swear,
he punish you.

130

And when you
make mad faces,
and that's
not nice.

If the President stop your car, the police is gonna run you over if you don't come.

When you, like, when you run and you turn around and you hit somebody else, you always gotta say "Sorry, and I won't do that again."

He make sures
nobody does
bad stuff.
(How does he do that?)
He has cameras.

132

When the
kids be mean,
he tells their
mom.

How does the President get around?

He probably has a limbo.

(Who drives it?)
This person.
He's a really fancy guy.
He opens doors for people.

134

It's a limbo driver.

I've seen a limbo before.
I've seen ten.

Once I saw a big black limo, and I think the President was in it.

(Who was driving?)
His uncle.

I know how that long car's called. It's a stretcher car.

He prob'ly doesn't
have his own airplane!
Airplanes don't park
in houses.
Otherwise they won't
fit in a garage.

136

They getta ride in
special cars and jets
and stuff.

He gots a red car and
one without the top
window.

I think he maybe, he might bring his horse 'cause it might to go potty.

[When it gets too cold] I think he'll ride in his carriage and go to, like, try to ask people if he can stay for the winter.

He has a
shiny car.
It's silver and
gold.

138

He drives
a monster
truck.

What else do you know about the President?

139

He grew up into a President.

George Washington is the boss of the President.

140

He's got a friend and his name is Gary.

He's given a watch to my brother. A cool one. It's Nike!

He's on quarters!

I know all the
President's names.
Lincoln's on the one cent.
Jefferson's on the five.
Roosevelt's on the ten
cents. Washington's on
twenty-five.

141

(Do all Presidents get to
be on money?)
The dead ones do.

He has bodyguards to protect him. They wear hard things. They go everywhere with him. They don't go into the bathroom with him.

But when he comes out they say, "Did you wash your hands, President?"

142

He doesn't work any
more because he died
and they put him on
the quarter.

George Washington,
he has a building
named after him.
George Washington, DC.

143

I know his number.
I think.

He has secret servants.

They're not secret, 'cause we all know about 'em.

144

They're on the top of the White House. Protecting the White House. When you look up, they disappear.

If the President gets
sick, the secret servant
is the President 'til he
get better.

I know him! He's
already dead, I think.

He gets ten dollars
a day.

He gots three hundred
dollars!

There's a lot more different Presidents.
I know another President.
George Lincoln.

146

The reptars ate him.

The President had to borrow some of my mom and dad's money to get some of that stuff.

kids tell us

My sister, she seen George Washington, and he gave my sister one dollar.

Today the President paid me back.

Fatherham Lincoln. He was our last President. He fighted in the Civil War.

They need to have fire because they got a basement.
They don't got light.

148

They go down there and write some stories down there.

The President got a whole office down there.

The President made
God, and then God
made the whole world.

He doesn't go to church
with me.
I used to go to church.
Now I'm five.

The President might
throw somebody in
the ocean and a whale
might save them.

He's in jail.

150

He can't go in jail because he's the President. He's the owner of the jail.

He's on the stone
with all the Presidents'
heads on it.

There's rocks sort of like
some of the Presidents
who died.

He's not alive.
They would take pictures
of him and then he gets to
be on the TV. They let the
tape rewind so then you
can see him again.

The two Presidents were not alive in the same day.

He got dead.
He got old.

152

Two of them got old.

When he died, he gets to be a statue.

He doesn't live in a white house. He lives up in heaven!!

He died. Then there's a statue in that building where he lived.

153

(When a new President is voted, does the old President have to move out of his house?)
No, because he's dead.

Abraham Lincoln
got shocked.

He can't help you
shovel snow because
he's dead. He's dead
a long time ago.

154

Abraham Lincoln is
the last one.
He's tall.
Like six-a-half.

He works in three big giant buildings hooked together. One's tall and two are the same size.

He has a book of pictures so he can remember when he was a baby.

The old one was the one that's on the quarter.

My brother has a placemat with all the Presidents on it.

156

(How many are there?)

Twenty.

He only works at night.

All the Presidents
used to live in the
White House.

(Does a President
live in the White
House now?)

NO!! HE'S DEAD!!

(Who lives in the
White House now?)

Nobody. It's empty.

But there's still
Presidents.

158

The guy who's on
the number one
bills dollar, he was
the first President.

(Is the guy who's
our President now
on any money?)

I think he's on the
two.

When is
it gonna be
over?

If you ask your own three to six-year-old these questions about the president and get some interesting answers, or, if you have a subject that you would like kids to tell us about, contact us at:

www.KidsTellUs.com

About the Authors

Warren Hanson is the illustrator of the classic "A Cup of Christmas Tea", as well as "Reading with Dad", "Tell Me What We Did Today", and several books about Peef, the colorful little bear. He has written and illustrated the comforting book "The Next Place", as well as "Older Love" and many others. He lives with his wife Patty in Saint Paul, Minnesota.

Tim Nyberg is the creator of the bestselling "Duct Tape Book" series, the 365 Days of Duct Tape Page-A-Day® Calendars, and "The Beanie Basher Handbook". He has co-authored "The WD-40 Book," "When I'm an Old Man, I'll Wear Mixed Plaids", "The Warning Label Book," "The Bubble Wrap Book,", "Rubber Chickens for the Soul," "Golf on the Tundra," "The Practical Joker's Handbook" and several other humor and parody books. He lives in Minnesota with his wife Julie.

Warren and Tim each have two delightful kids who were the age of the kids quoted in this book nearly two decades ago.